I0755700

Date

A SOUL INSPIRED PRAYER JOURNAL

JANA KENNEDY-SPICER

featuring

BETSY DE CRUZ

SWEET TO THE SOUL PRESS

# DEDICATION

To my aunts
- Maggie, Letha, Mildred, Ola Mae, Offie -
the inspiring women in my life.

Your prayers over your children, grand-children,
nieces and nephews, have protected us more
than we will ever know.

*Thank you.*

***Pray Relentlessly —A Soul Inspired Prayer Journal***

Second Edition, Revised

www.SweetToTheSoul.com

ISBN: 978-1-953718-04-4

Sweet To The Soul Press
PO Box 785
Royse City, Tx 75189

Original hand lettering by: Jana Kennedy-Spicer
Cover design and interior layout by: Jana Kennedy-Spicer



To order additional copies of this book and access additional resources, visit www.sweetothesoul.com/inspiring-women.htm

To inquire about ordering in quantities of 10 or more, please email info@sweettothesoul.com

# CONTENTS

# SCRIPTURE READING LIST

- ☐ 1 Thessalonians 5:16-18
- ☐ Philippians 4:6-7
- ☐ 1 John 5:14
- ☐ Colossians 4:2
- ☐ Mark 11:24
- ☐ Jeremiah 29:12
- ☐ Romans 12:12
- ☐ Matthew 6:7
- ☐ Psalm 145:18
- ☐ Jeremiah 33:3
- ☐ Hebrews 4:16
- ☐ Matthew 6:6
- ☐ Psalm 18:6
- ☐ 1 John 5:15
- ☐ James 1:6
- ☐ James 5:16
- ☐ Luke 6:27-28
- ☐ Acts 16:25
- ☐ Acts 1:14
- ☐ 1 Peter 4:7
- ☐ John 15:16
- ☐ John 14:13
- ☐ Romans 8:26
- ☐ Matthew 21:22
- ☐ Psalm 118:5
- ☐ Philippians 1:19
- ☐ Psalm 5:3
- ☐ Psalm 42:8
- ☐ Psalm 143:1
- ☐ Matthew 5:44
- ☐ Acts 13:3

Rejoice
always,
PRAY
Relentlessly
Give Thanks in
all circumstances

FOR THIS IS THE WILL
OF GOD IN CHRIST JESUS
FOR YOU

1 Thessalonians 5:16-18

# INTRODUCTION

## PRAYER.

I have to admit, this word has always intimidated me. I spent many years feeling inadequate and unworthy to come before God with my petitions. Fumbling through the right words, careful to try and say just the right thing. For some reason thinking I had to silently pray in the "King James Version".

It was a struggle, so I would find myself there only as a last resort.

I spent so much time thinking that prayer was just a way to ask God for what I wanted, never understanding that prayer served a much greater purpose. I never really grasped that God loves me and wanted to have a relationship with me.

Of course, to build a relationship with someone takes time. It demands spending time with each other. And maybe most important, it requires communication.

Prayer.

## Prayer Warrior or Prayer Wimp?

Hello, I'm Jana, and I'm a prayer wimp.

In Max Lucado's book, "*Before Amen*", he starts off with this:

*"Hello, my name is Max. I'm a recovering prayer wimp. I doze off when I pray. My thoughts zig, then zag, then zig again. Distractions swarm like gnats on a summer night. If attention deficit disorder applies to prayer, I am afflicted. When I pray, I think of a thousand things I need to do. I forget the one thing I set out to do. Pray."*

Does this sound familiar to you?

It is so me! I can be there talking to God, journaling what is on my heart and then I remember that we need milk. Or that I forgot to call someone back. And is that pizza from last night in the fridge, because now I need a snack.

If you know me, I'm sure you are not surprised because conversations with me kind of flow the same way.

I must admit it is a bit comforting to know that a pastor and man of God such as Max Lucado has struggled with prayer also.

Somehow knowing I am not alone tells me there is hope for me! And friend if you are saying, "yea, that sounds like me too", then know that there is hope for you also!

## A Conversation

I had never thought of prayer as a conversation between myself and God. I was intimidated. How do you have a conversation with the creator of the universe? Why would He want to talk to me?

A conversation seems personal, confidential, mutual. Yes a conversation is all of those things and that is part of the beauty of prayer. *God wants to be personal with us.*

We are told in Hebrews 4:14-16 that God is approachable:

**"Since then we have a great high priest who has passed through the heavens, Jesus, the Son of God, let us hold fast our confession. For we do not have a high priest who is unable to sympathize with our weaknesses, but one who in every respect has been tempted as we are, yet without sin. Let us then with confidence draw near to the throne of grace, that we may receive mercy and find grace to help in time of need."**

This is a wonderful encouragement for us!

In Old Testament days, there was a section of the tabernacle which housed the Ark of the Covenant, the early dwelling place of God's earthly presence. This Holy of Holies was separated by a tall thick veil, or curtain. No one could enter this sacred chamber except the high priest and he only entered once a year on the Day of Atonement. On that day, the High Priest would make intercession for sin on behalf of the people.

The veil represented the separation of man from God because of our sin. At Christ's death, that separation was removed, and mankind could have direct access to God the Father, as symbolized by the tearing of the thick and heavy veil.

**"And Jesus cried out again with a loud voice and yielded up his spirit. And behold, the curtain of the temple was torn in two, from top to bottom. And the earth shook, and the rocks were split."** Matthew 27:50-51

Yes Christ's sacrifice took away this veil. Christians today, with the indwelling of the Holy Spirit, have direct access to God the Father, and are not separated from Him as if by a veil.

Friends this is such a gift!

## Progress

If I am honest with you, I still consider myself a bit of a prayer wimp. I am not where I want to be, and not where I think I need to be, but with God's help, I am not where I used to be. *Progress.*

One thing which helps me is writing down my prayers, journaling my prayers. You may already use this practice also, but if not I want to encourage you to journal about your time with God.

My friend Karmen Smith is an avid prayer journaler, and in her book *"When You Pray Big Things Happen"*, tells us *"I wish I could put my finger on the day journaling changed for me. All I know is that when I did start journaling for real, my life changed. I've been an avid journaler for a little over a decade. Journaling has allowed me to purge my soul of toxic emotions. Some journal entries have been peaceful, while others were so full of pain that I actually tore the page as I wrote. There have been pages of praise and pages full of questions for God."*

## In This Journal

In this prayer journal, *"Pray Relentlessly"*, we are going to take a deeper look into what God's Word has to reveal to us about why and how we are to pray.

Included in these pages you will find a daily **Scripture Reading List** with 31 verses meant to encourage you in developing a daily habit of prayer. You will read encouragements for your own prayers, Biblical accounts of other's prayers, and scriptures which teach us how we should pray.

In **Propelled to Pray**, we dig into the Scriptures to learn how our faith in God moves us to spend timed with Him in prayer.

Betsy DeCruz joins us to talk about one of my favorite methods of prayer, **Praying Scripture** and discover the sections of God's Word which we can pray back to Him for many situations.

In **Lord, Teach Us To Pray**, we will learn prayer is so much more than just asking God for the things we want as we discuss the five principles of prayer as Jesus taught His disciple how to pray. pray.

You will also find many pages available for you to journal your personal prayers as you study through this Prayer Journal.

Friends, my prayer for you is that *Pray Relentlessly* will encourage you in the building of a daily habit of prayer and the deepening of a relationship with God.

My personal prayer for me is that as I study through this prayer journal myself, that it will stretch my prayer muscles and that the woman I am when I close this journal is not the same as the one who opened it.

*Father God, thank You for the great privilege to meet with you through prayer. The idea that You want to have relationship with us is humbling and quite astounding. Father, I ask you today to give each of us a desire to sit at your feet, a desire to build relationship with you and a hunger that only prayer can satisfy. In Jesus's name, Amen*

Blessings Soul Friends, Jana

## Make A Plan

In the space below take a few minutes to talk to God and set your own personal goal using this journal. Then identify 3 specific actions you can take to help achieve this goal.

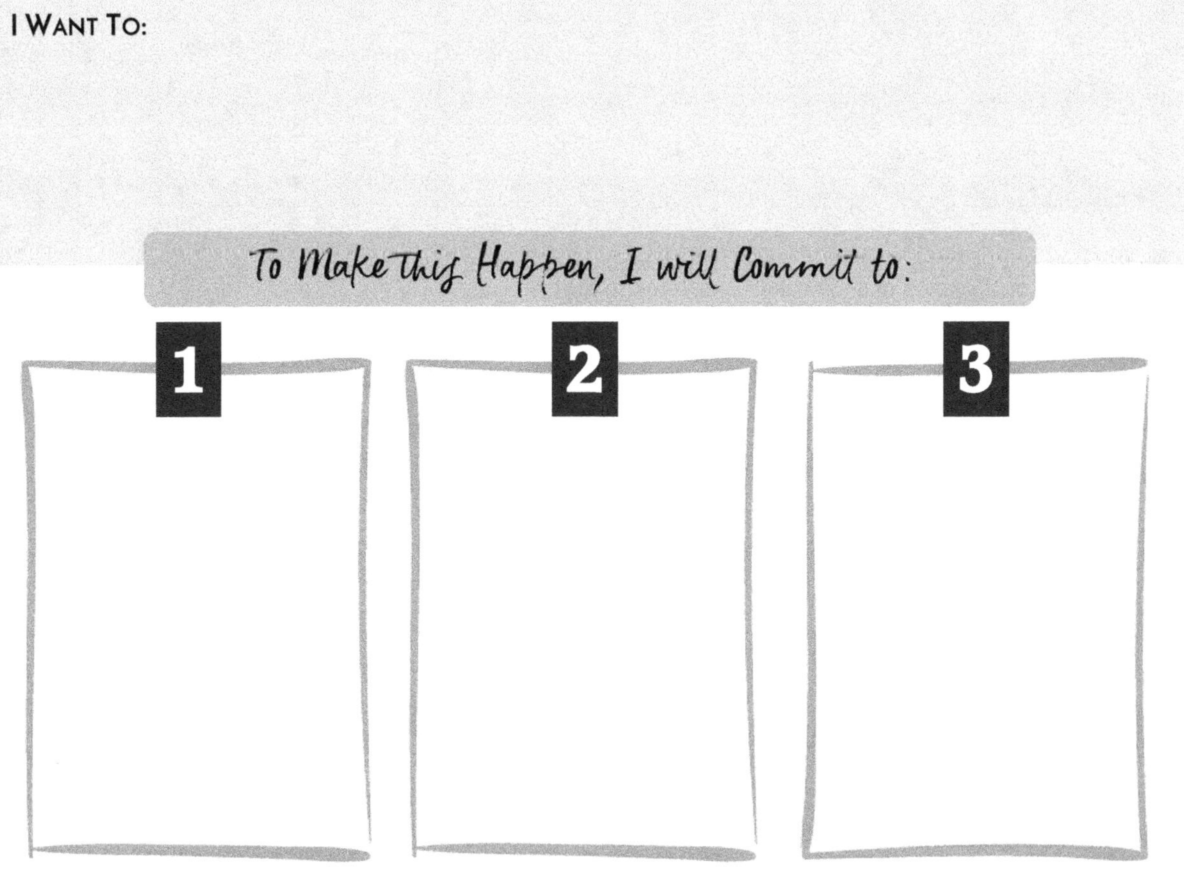

## DATE:

## SCRIPTURE:

- Ask God to reveal a Scripture to pray or select one from your Bible reading.
- Write it out in this section.

## PRAISE:

- This section of prayer time is all about God.
- Begin your prayer time by praising God for who He is. Pray Scripture back to Him which gives Him praise and honor—Psalm is a good source for these scriptures. Acknowledge the way you have seen God working in your life or in the lives of others.

## FOR OTHERS:

- This next section of prayer time is devoted to others.
- Keep a list of names and their needs, update God in your prayer time. Petition God on behalf of your friends and family just as if you were talking to a friend for them. This type of prayer is called intercessory prayer—you are interceding with God on their behalf.

## FOR ME:

- This time with God, talk to Him about your personal needs.
- Physical, spiritual, emotional, anything. Open up, be honest, He knows your heart anyway. Talk to Him about your day, your relationships, your challenges, your hopes, your everything.

## THANKSGIVING:

- This section of your prayer time is all about thanksgiving.
- Everything is from God, so acknowledge Him for all He has provided. Large and small, physical and spiritual, everything comes from Him.

## GOD'S RESPONSE:

- Lastly, sit and listen for God's response.
- Notate what He might be prompting you to do or come back at a later time and make a note about how God has answered today's prayers.

DATE:

SCRIPTURE:

PRAISE:

FOR OTHERS:

**FOR ME:**

**THANKSGIVING:**

**GOD'S RESPONSE:**

DATE:

SCRIPTURE:

PRAISE:

FOR OTHERS:

## FOR ME:

## THANKSGIVING:

## GOD'S RESPONSE:

DATE:

SCRIPTURE:

PRAISE:

FOR OTHERS:

## FOR ME:

## THANKSGIVING:

## GOD'S RESPONSE:

DATE:

SCRIPTURE:

PRAISE:

FOR OTHERS:

## FOR ME:

## THANKSGIVING:

## GOD'S RESPONSE:

**DATE:**

**SCRIPTURE:**

**PRAISE:**

**FOR OTHERS:**

## FOR ME:

## THANKSGIVING:

## GOD'S RESPONSE:

DATE:

SCRIPTURE:

PRAISE:

FOR OTHERS:

**FOR ME:**

**THANKSGIVING:**

**GOD'S RESPONSE:**

DATE:

SCRIPTURE:

PRAISE:

FOR OTHERS:

**FOR ME:**

**THANKSGIVING:**

**GOD'S RESPONSE:**

# PRAYER NEEDS

Name: ______________________________

Need: ______________________________

______________________________

______________________________

Name: ______________________________

Need: ______________________________

______________________________

______________________________

Name: ______________________________

Need: ______________________________

______________________________

______________________________

Name: ______________________________

Need: ______________________________

______________________________

______________________________

Name: ______________________________

Need: ______________________________

______________________________

______________________________

Name: ______________________________

Need: ______________________________

______________________________

______________________________

Name: ______________________________

Need: ______________________________

______________________________

______________________________

Name: ______________________________

Need: ______________________________

______________________________

______________________________

Name: ______________________________

Need: ______________________________

______________________________

______________________________

Name: ______________________________

Need: ______________________________

______________________________

______________________________

Name: ______________________________

Need: ______________________________

______________________________

______________________________

Name: ______________________________

Need: ______________________________

______________________________

______________________________

Name: ______________________________

Need: ______________________________

______________________________

______________________________

Name: ______________________________

Need: ______________________________

______________________________

______________________________

# PRAYER NEEDS

Name: ____________________________________________

Need: ____________________________________________

__________________________________________________

__________________________________________________

Name: ____________________________________________

Need: ____________________________________________

__________________________________________________

__________________________________________________

Name: ____________________________________________

Need: ____________________________________________

__________________________________________________

__________________________________________________

Name: ____________________________________________

Need: ____________________________________________

__________________________________________________

__________________________________________________

Name: ____________________________________________

Need: ____________________________________________

__________________________________________________

__________________________________________________

Name: ____________________________________________

Need: ____________________________________________

__________________________________________________

__________________________________________________

Name: ____________________________________________

Need: ____________________________________________

__________________________________________________

__________________________________________________

Name: ______________________________________________

Need: ______________________________________________

____________________________________________________

____________________________________________________

Name: ______________________________________________

Need: ______________________________________________

____________________________________________________

____________________________________________________

Name: ______________________________________________

Need: ______________________________________________

____________________________________________________

____________________________________________________

Name: ______________________________________________

Need: ______________________________________________

____________________________________________________

____________________________________________________

Name: ______________________________________________

Need: ______________________________________________

____________________________________________________

____________________________________________________

Name: ______________________________________________

Need: ______________________________________________

____________________________________________________

____________________________________________________

Name: ______________________________________________

Need: ______________________________________________

____________________________________________________

____________________________________________________

Then Jesus looked up and said,

thank you

"Father, I thank you that you have heard me."

John 11:41

Thank you Father that you hear our cries;
that you listen to every prayer we offer,
whether fitfully spoken or muffled & mumbled
through broken hearts and flowing tears.

Lord God, thank you for the gift of the Holy Spirit,
so that in those moments when we
do not know what to speak, when
words cannot be verbalized even in the heart,
that the Holy Spirit does intercede and
petition for us and, yes,
you hear those precious prayers also.

Whether whispered quietly on our knees
or shouted boldly on our feet,
you hear our prayer.
Whether we are alone or gathered with many,
you hear our prayer.
Whether at the alter or the bedside or the graveside,
you meet us wherever we are
and you hear our prayer.

Thank you Father for this gift of prayer,
of being able to meet with you,
to speak directly to you,
at any time, in any place,
under any condition.

And thank you Lord that you hear every word,
every time from every one.

*In Jesus' Name, Amen*

# PROPELLED TO PRAY

## Why Do We Pray?

As a youth in church, I asked this question often. I could understand that prayer had its place *in church*, but I must admit I struggled to find its place outside of church in my daily life.

But now, being much older, when I read "why do we pray" I think, why *don't* we pray?

When my kids arrived at the age to get a job, I began encouraging them to save some of that paycheck each week. Of course they were excited to have money of their own and didn't really want mom's advice on how to spend it. Flash forward several years and their saving habits have allowed them to purchase their own homes, vehicles, etc.

At the age of 16 they could not see the value of their mom's advice. They didn't yet understand that advice was coming from a place of experience. Mom knew the value of saving money.

So as a youth myself when my church leaders would encourage me to develop a habit of praying daily, I couldn't really see the true value.

Today, having a few more gray hairs and having been delivered by God through many storms, I much more understand the value of spending time with God in prayer.

Have I developed a strong practice of daily prayer? Not exactly (remember the "Introduction"?) but I'm working on it. And thankfully God is patient with me. Spiritual growth is a constant throughout our life. Just like our physical bodies, there are times of great growth and times when the growing happens a little slower. Yet, we keep growing ever closer to God.

Whatever season of growth you are in friend, I encourage you to keep praying. Keep talking to God. Keep listening to God. And if you need a little encouragement right now, read though what God's Word has to teach us about the following three reasons why we pray.

☐ Before you flip the page and continue reading, pause for a few minutes and answer this question: ***What moves you to pray?***

## WHY DO WE PRAY? BECAUSE: FAITH

The most basic of all reason's Christian's pray, is because they have faith. Faith in God that He is who He says He is. Faith that God loves and hears us when we pray. Faith that God will answer our prayers.

There are literally countless things we may pray for, but before we even get any words out, we bend our hearts to a position of prayer because of our faith in God.

I have often said that faith is a verb. It's not a thing we have, it is something that we do. Faith is not docile, it is active. Faith incites us to move. Faith propels us to pray.

## 1 FAITH IN GOD: *That He is who He says He is*

### I AM WHO I AM

In Exodus Moses asked God a simple enough question, 'what is your name?'.

> ***GOD SAID TO MOSES, "I AM WHO I AM". AND HE SAID, "SAY THIS TO THE PEOPLE OF ISRAEL, 'I AM HAS SENT ME TO YOU.'"*** Exodus 3:14

The statement "I AM" comes from the Hebrew verb "to be or to exist." With this statement, God declared that He is self-existent, eternal, self-sufficient, self-directed, and unchanging.

This response set God apart from all foreign gods some people may have known and worshiped. This God was not formed by human hands nor named by human language.

God's statement also declared that He is present. Despite his different nature and not being man-made, God is always present with his people.

Revealing this holy name to Moses also shows an intimate relationship, being on a first name basis with the God of the universe.

### CREATOR OF THE UNIVERSE

> ***"IN THE BEGINNING, GOD CREATED THE HEAVENS AND THE EARTH."*** Genesis 1:1

There may be people who want to debate theories about the creation of our world, but the Bible is clear: *God created it all and in such an order to make the earth his dwelling place.*

When you read Genesis chapters 1:1—2:3 you will see an sequence which 'conveys the picture of the all-powerful, transcendent God who sets everything in place with consummate skill in conformity to his grand design.' (ESV Study Bible)

God had a plan and he still has a plan. As we travel this earth, we are part of God's plan. Our time on earth is not by mistake. The people in our lives are not by accident.

## Alpha and Omega

***"I am the Alpha and the Omega, the First and the Last, the Beginning and the End."***

Revelation 22:13

God was before all time, he formed the world and he will be the one to bring it to it's end. God originated the plan of salvation and he will be the one to bring it to completion.

If God is the beginning and the end, then friends, he is also all the in-between. He is in everything. I don't mean that in some cosmological new-age theory, but in the sense that God is in control of every thing that happens. Large or small, difficult or easy.

God has a purpose and a plan in everything. And although at times it may not seem like it, God is ultimately in control of all things.

## Diving Deeper

☐ Look up each of the scriptures below, then notate in the corresponding box, what that scripture reveals to us about who God is.

| |
|---|
| Isaiah 42:5 |
| Isaiah 45:18 |
| 1 John 4:8 |
| Colossians 1:16 |
| John 4:24 |
| 1 Timothy 1:17 |
| John 1:1 |

# 2 FAITH IN GOD: *That He Loves us & Hears our Prayers*

## God So Loved Us

As sure as God's love for us began before time [*he created this world to inhabit it with us*], the enemy has been trying to separate us from God's love for just as long. The serpent's words to Eve, "*did God really say*?" (Genesis 3:1) triggered her doubt and caused a ripple effect through all the generations which continues today.

But God himself reassures of his love for us through his Word.

☐ How do each of these scriptures define God's love?

John 3:16

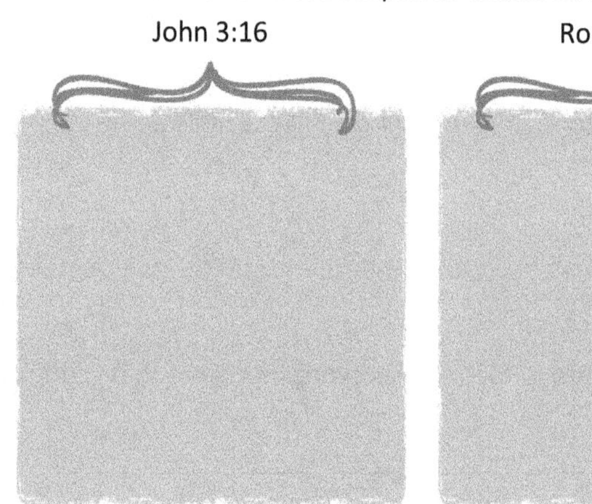

Romans 5:8

1 John 4:10

It is important to base our understanding of God's love on the truth of his Word and not on our feelings or circumstances. The fact that God loves us is stated over and over in the Bible.

☐ Look up each of the scriptures below and match them with the corresponding description of God's love.

| | |
|---|---|
| a) God's love surpasses knowledge | s) 1 John 3:1 |
| b) God's love is everlasting | t) Psalm 136:26 |
| c) God's love is steadfast | u) John 15:13 |
| d) God loves us as his own children | v) Ephesians 3:19 |
| e) God's love makes him merciful and life-giving | w) Psalm 103:17 |
| f) God's love is the greatest of all loves | x) Romans 8:37-39 |
| g) God's love endures forever | y) Jeremiah 31:3 |
| h) Nothing can separate us from God's love | z) Ephesians 2:4-5 |

☐ Which one of these scriptures reassures your heart the most and why?

## God Hears Our Prayers

One of the key faith components to prayer must be that we *believe* God hears our prayers. Otherwise, why would we pray? We may wonder, sometimes, if we do not receive an answer right away or receive an answer other than the one we want, but we can be reassured that God does hear our prayers because the Bible tells us so.

*"But I call to God, and the **LORD** will save me. Evening and morning and at noon I utter my complaint and moan, and he hears my voice."*
Psalm 55:16-17

As we mature spiritually, our prayers grow from random requests for things we want into deeper, personal, real conversations. We may begin with ATM prayers, you know, when we only talk to God when we want something, but the more time we spend with God in prayer, the more we develop a relationship. We know He is listening to our prayers.

You may be reading the scripture above and be thinking, of course God would listen to King David, the *'man after God's own heart'* (1 Samuel 13:14) but why would God listen to me? I know I have thought this a lot! Especially when I have been away from him for a period of time.

⇒ **Nothing is hidden from God**, even our thoughts, hopes and dreams when we do not utter them, God knows. (Hebrews 4:13) I think we sometimes confuse God not answering our prayers the way we want with God not hearing our prayers.

⇒ **The Bible gives evidence** of God listening to and answering the prayers of others. When I am having a hard time seeing the proof in my situation, I look at how God has listened to prior generations.

☐ How did God respond to the prayers of each of these people?

Sarah's Prayer for a child (Genesis 16:11)

Moses on Mount Sinai (Deuteronomy 9:19)

David crying out for deliverance (2 Samuel 22:7)

Israel's groans under slavery (Exodus 2:24)

Zachariah's prayer for a miracle (Luke 1:13-14)

☐ Recall a time when God answered one of your own prayers.

We can’t close out this section without recognizing that there *is* something which will prevent God from hearing our prayers. The same thing that separates us from God also blocks our prayers.

☐ Look up each of the following scriptures and make a notation of what we are told will prevent God from hearing our prayers.

☐ Psalm 66:18

☐ John 9:31

☐ 1 Peter 3:12

☐ Proverbs 28:9

☐ Isaiah 1:15-17

☐ Proverbs 15:29

## HeartCheck

Have you been feeling like God is not hearing your prayers? Is there any undealt with sin in your life? Pause and take some time here to sit and talk to God. No formalities. No pretense. Just a willingness to be open and honest and to hear God's response.

☐ Be brave enough to ask God to point out any sin which you need to confess.

☐ Ask him for strength to break the chains of any habitual sin in your life.

☐ Thank him for his grace and mercy and forgiveness.

☐ Praise him for his redemption which washes away our sins.

## 3 FAITH IN GOD: *That He will Answer our Prayers*

### THE CHURCH PRAYS FOR PETER (READ ACTS 12)

In Acts chapter 12, we read an account which seems to play right out of one of today's novels. In short, James, the apostle, has just been killed by King Herod Agrippa, who is the grandson of Herod the Great. He also has Peter imprisoned with the intent of killing him as well.

"***SO PETER WAS KEPT IN PRISON, BUT EARNEST PRAYER FOR HIM WAS MADE TO GOD BY THE CHURCH.***" Acts 12:5

What type of prayer?

- ☐ Look up the Bible verse Acts 12:5 in various translations and list the word(s) each used to describe the church's prayer. (BibleHub.com is a great resource for this.)
  - ⇒ NIV—New International Version ______
  - ⇒ BSB—Berean Study Bible ______
  - ⇒ KJV—King James Version ______
  - ⇒ NKJV—New King James Version ______
  - ⇒ NASB—New American Standard Bible ______
  - ⇒ (other) ______

- ☐ What can we learn from the church's example of prayer?

They say "Desperate times call for desperate measures" and for Christians, that means desperate prayers. Not a casual mention, but fervent, earnest, intense, constant prayer. The friends at Mary's house were praying until their prayers were answered—*literally*.

Knowing this causes me to wonder, how often do we not receive God's answer to prayer because we simply give up praying?

**PRAY. THEN PRAY AGAIN. THEN PRAY SOME MORE.**
**AND CONTINUE TO PRAY UNTIL GOD'S ANSWER ARRIVES.**

- ☐ Do you have a desperate need in your life which requires desperate prayer?

## Daniel and His Friends, Seek Mercy (Read Daniel 2)

The book of Daniel is one of my absolute favorites. Full of intrigue, drama, history, miracles, angels, oh my. In chapter 2 we learn about the first of many dreams for King Nebuchadnezzar. Dreams which he nor any of his "magicians, enchanters and sorcerers" (v.2) could understand. So King Neb, orders all of his "wise men" to be put to death. Among whom were a young Daniel and his three friends Hananiah, Mishael and Azariah, who all certainly did not want to die.

"***Then Daniel went to his house ... and told them to seek mercy from the God of heaven concerning this mystery, so that Daniel and his companions might not be destroyed with the rest of Babylon.***" Daniel 2:17-18

Who prayed? "Them".

☐ Who did Daniel implore to pray with him?

Daniel could clearly see the dire need at hand and fully recognized that it would take an action of God to deliver them from this murderous order from the King. But Daniel was also aware of the power of unified prayer.

"***Again I say to you, if two of you agree on earth about anything they ask, it will be done for them by my Father in heaven. For where two or three are gathered in my name, there am I among them.***"

Matthew 18:19-20.

Let's look at some characteristics of unified prayer.

### Everyone in Agreement

- The first key to unified prayer is for everyone to be unified in what they are praying for. This also means they must be unified in faith as well. Faith for the thing they are praying about and belief that God will answer their prayer. Without this faith, there is no agreement.
- The second key to unified prayer is for there to be no division amongst those praying. It is hard to pray in a unified fashion—even when all agree on the need—if there is any division or disagreement between any of the group members.

### Jesus at the Center

- In order for God to fulfill any request we are making, it must be in alignment with His will. We may not always know if the answer we are seeking is exactly how God wants to respond to the specific situation. However, we can be sure if what we are asking is *outside* of God's will if it *does not align with His Word*.

- We must also remember that it is Jesus in the midst of us, those praying, which gives power to our prayers. When we are gathered in His name to pray for His will, He is among us.

### Answered Prayer

Theologian Andrew Murray has said, "The mark that there has been true united prayer is the fruit, the answer, the receiving of the thing for which we asked." We see this fulfilled for both of the groups of people praying in our Scripture examples.

- "The church" in Acts prayed for Peter's freedom and God sent an angel to deliver him from jail. Daniel and his friends prayed for God's mercy and God spared their lives by giving Daniel understanding of the King's dream.
- Did you notice how God answered their prayers? It was miraculous! God's answer to their prayers left no doubt that it was indeed from Him and not orchestrated by man.

### Heartcheck

Has God been speaking to you through this section? He has me, convicting me really.

☐ Do you have Christian friends you can call on for unified prayer?

☐ Are <u>you</u> a praying friend someone can call on for unified prayer? How can you support your friends and family through prayer?

☐ What do you sense God wanting you to learn about His ability and willingness to answer your prayers?

DATE:

SCRIPTURE:

PRAISE:

FOR OTHERS:

**FOR ME:**

**THANKSGIVING:**

**GOD'S RESPONSE:**

DATE:

SCRIPTURE:

PRAISE:

FOR OTHERS:

## FOR ME:

## THANKSGIVING:

## GOD'S RESPONSE:

**DATE:**

**SCRIPTURE:**

**PRAISE:**

**FOR OTHERS:**

FOR ME:

THANKSGIVING:

GOD'S RESPONSE:

DATE:

SCRIPTURE:

PRAISE:

FOR OTHERS:

## FOR ME:

## THANKSGIVING:

## GOD'S RESPONSE:

DATE:

SCRIPTURE:

PRAISE:

FOR OTHERS:

## FOR ME:

## THANKSGIVING:

## GOD'S RESPONSE:

DATE:

SCRIPTURE:

PRAISE:

FOR OTHERS:

## FOR ME:

## THANKSGIVING:

## GOD'S RESPONSE:

DATE:

SCRIPTURE:

PRAISE:

FOR OTHERS:

## FOR ME:

## THANKSGIVING:

## GOD'S RESPONSE:

# PRAYER NEEDS

Name: ______________________________________________

Need: ______________________________________________

______________________________________________

______________________________________________

Name: ______________________________________________

Need: ______________________________________________

______________________________________________

______________________________________________

Name: ______________________________________________

Need: ______________________________________________

______________________________________________

______________________________________________

Name: ______________________________________________

Need: ______________________________________________

______________________________________________

______________________________________________

Name: ______________________________________________

Need: ______________________________________________

______________________________________________

______________________________________________

Name: ______________________________________________

Need: ______________________________________________

______________________________________________

______________________________________________

Name: ______________________________________________

Need: ______________________________________________

______________________________________________

______________________________________________

Name: ____________________

Need: ____________________

____________________

____________________

Name: ____________________

Need: ____________________

____________________

____________________

Name: ____________________

Need: ____________________

____________________

____________________

Name: ____________________

Need: ____________________

____________________

____________________

Name: ____________________

Need: ____________________

____________________

____________________

Name: ____________________

Need: ____________________

____________________

____________________

Name: ____________________

Need: ____________________

____________________

____________________

# PRAYER NEEDS

Name: ______________________________

Need: ______________________________

______________________________

______________________________

Name: ______________________________

Need: ______________________________

______________________________

______________________________

Name: ______________________________

Need: ______________________________

______________________________

______________________________

Name: ______________________________

Need: ______________________________

______________________________

______________________________

Name: ______________________________

Need: ______________________________

______________________________

______________________________

Name: ______________________________

Need: ______________________________

______________________________

______________________________

Name: ______________________________

Need: ______________________________

______________________________

______________________________

Name: ___

Need: ___

___

___

Name: ___

Need: ___

___

___

Name: ___

Need: ___

___

___

Name: ___

Need: ___

___

___

Name: ___

Need: ___

___

___

Name: ___

Need: ___

___

___

Name: ___

Need: ___

___

___

have mercy on me O God

## David's Prayer of Repentance

Have mercy on me, O God,
according to your steadfast love;
according to your abundant mercy
blot out my transgressions.
Wash me thoroughly from my iniquity,
and cleanse me from my sin!

For I know my transgressions,
and my sin is ever before me.
Against you, you only, have I sinned
and done what is evil in your sight,
so that you may be justified in your words
and blameless in your judgment.
Behold, I was brought forth in iniquity,
and in sin did my mother conceive me.
Behold, you delight in truth in the inward being,
and you teach me wisdom in the secret heart.

Purge me with hyssop, and I shall be clean;
wash me, and I shall be whiter than snow.
Let me hear joy and gladness;
let the bones that you have broken rejoice.
Hide your face from my sins,
and blot out all my iniquities.
Create in me a clean heart, O God,
and renew a right spirit within me.
Cast me not away from your presence,
and take not your Holy Spirit from me.
Restore to me the joy of your salvation,
and uphold me with a willing spirit.

Psalm 51:1-12

# PRAYING SCRIPTURE

BETSY DE CRUZ

Do you ever feel unsure of how to pray for someone you love? Have you ever gotten tired of praying the same things day in and day out? Does your mind wonder while you're trying to talk to God?

Friend, you are not alone. I'm the queen of distraction, so I've experienced all of these. I want to grow closer to God and see lives changed through prayer, yet my mind can travel to the moon and back when I try to pray. That's why I want to learn more about using God's Word to fuel and focus my conversation with Him.

**SCRIPTURE WORKS LIKE A SPRINGBOARD FOR PRAYER.**

As we read it, the Holy Spirit sparks our thoughts and leads us into closer communion with Him.

## PRAYING GOD'S WORD HAS SEVERAL BENEFITS:

- **It gives direction to our prayer.** When we don't know how to pray for a person or situation, Scripture show us. We know we're praying in line with God's will when we pray His very words back to Him. And when we're left speechless at the end of our rope, it gives us the words we need.
- **God's Word has power.** Scripture has authority. It's alive and active. It's a mighty weapon of spiritual warfare that fuels our faith and breaks down strongholds. We find power when we pray God's Inspired Word.
- **God's Word is an anchor.** When your mind wonders, you can always go back to the Scripture that sparked your prayer. When your faith flounders, the Bible gives you words to declare and something to stand on.

## THREE WAYS TO PRAY USING SCRIPTURE:

1. **Pray God's Word in Your Quiet Time**
   In your devotional reading, respond to God's words by praying them back to Him. After you read a passage, go back and read it again, pausing to respond to God when you see a verse that sparks prayer.

   Look for the following:
   > A quality or action you can praise God for.
   > A blessing to thank Him for.
   > Something you want to ask God for.

2. **Use memory verses as prayer prompts.**
   If you're using a Scripture memory program, spend a few minutes praying through a verse after you review it. Lift up to God whatever

thoughts come to mind. Perhaps you'll want to pray for yourself or for a loved one, asking for grace to obey a command, or faith to believe a promise.

3. **Pray along with the prayers of the Bible.**
   God's Word contains the most beautiful and powerful prayers ever written. Pray along with the people of the Bible as they wrestle with God, praise Him, and bring their petitions before Him.

   Here are several prayers from Scripture you can make your own:
   > 1 Corinthians 29:10-13
   > Psalm 51
   > Luke 1:46-55
   > Ephesians 1:15-23
   > Ephesians 3:14-21
   > Colossians 1:9-12

**As you pray more of God's Word, your faith will grow.** When your words echo His, you grow closer to Him. Soul Friends, here's something you can try right now before you go.

☐ Read 1 John 1:5
*"This is the message we have heard from him and proclaim to you, that God is light, and in him is no darkness."*

☐ Do you know someone who needs to know this right now? Stop a moment to pray for that person and praise God for His guiding light.

# PRAYER WALL SCRIPTURES

I love Betsy's method of praying scripture so much that I have searched the Bible for scriptures to pray over my family, and over some specific topical needs.

Over the next few pages you will find some of these scriptures printed out on note cards which you can cut out from this journal. Use them to pin up in your private prayer space. Or tuck them in your Bible or journal to use during your quiet time with God.

- >> For children, Colossians 1:9-14
- >> For married couples, Romans 15:5-6
- >> For men, Ephesians 6:11-18
- >> For women, Proverbs 31:25-31
- >> For parents, Ephesians 1:15-20
- >> For spouses, 1 Corinthians 13:4-13
- >> For friends, Ephesians 3:14-19
- >> For ourself, Luke 1:46-55
- >> For confidence, 2 Corinthians 3:4-6
- >> Forgiving others, Matthew 6:14-15
- >> For repentance, Psalm 51
- >> Attitude, Colossians 3:12-13
- >> Thanksgiving, 1 Chronicles 16:34
- >> For endurance, Hebrews 12:1-2
- >> Peace keeping, Titus 3:1-2
- >> Worry, Philippians 4:4-7

☐ What additional Scriptures can you add to this list?

## Personalizing Scripture

When I use Scripture to pray over others, I use the verse as a guide and personalize with the person's name and even add in any specifics related to their situation or current conditions.

Here is an example using Romans 15:5-6. All of our children are adults now and I love praying this over the married couples.

> *Father, you are the God of endurance and encouragement and I ask you to guide and support Marty and Jana during this time of crisis. Enable them to work through any circumstances of disagreement and find harmony together with you. Let them live this out in such a way to bear witness to your goodness and may You be glorified above all else. In Jesus' name, Amen*

If one of them have made me aware of any specific conflict or issue, I will even insert those circumstances into my prayer. I have even prayed this Scripture over my own marriage.

I love how Betsy mentioned that "Scripture works like a springboard for prayer." Using Scripture as a starting point, my prayers seem to take off and flow into a natural conversation for my time with God.

☐ Now it's your turn. Select one of the Scriptures from the list on the previous page and write out a personalized prayer for someone below.

Clip each prayer card to add to your prayer wall, Bible or journal. You can add the name of the person you are praying for and notes on the back of each card.

*Praying For:* ____________

Strength and dignity are her clothing, and she laughs at the time to come. She opens her mouth with wisdom, and the teaching of kindness is on her tongue. She looks well to the ways of her household and does not eat the bread of idleness. Her children rise up and call her blessed; her husband also, and he praises her: "Many women have done excellently, but you surpass them all." Charm is deceitful, and beauty is vain, but a woman who fears the LORD is to be praised. Give her of the fruit of her hands, and let her works praise her in the gates.

Proverbs 31:25-31

*Praying For:* ____________

**MAY THE GOD OF ENDURANCE AND ENCOURAGEMENT GRANT YOU TO LIVE IN SUCH HARMONY WITH ONE ANOTHER, IN ACCORD WITH CHRIST JESUS, THAT TOGETHER YOU MAY WITH ONE VOICE GLORIFY THE GOD AND FATHER OF OUR LORD JESUS CHRIST.**

**ROMANS 15:5-6**

*Praying For:* ____________

Put on the whole armor of God, that you may be able to stand against the schemes of the devil. For we do not wrestle against flesh and blood, but against the rulers, against the authorities, against the cosmic powers over this present darkness, against the spiritual forces of evil in the heavenly places. Therefore take up the whole armor of God, that you may be able to withstand in the evil day, and having done all, to stand firm. Stand therefore, having fastened on the belt of truth, and having put on the breastplate of righteousness, and, as shoes for your feet, having put on the readiness given by the gospel of peace. In all circumstances take up the shield of faith, with which you can extinguish all the flaming darts of the evil one; and take the helmet of salvation, and the sword of the Spirit, which is the word of God, praying at all times in the Spirit, with all prayer and supplication. To that end, keep alert with all perseverance, making supplication for all the saints.

Ephesians 6:11-18

Praying For: __________

And so, from the day we heard, we have not ceased to pray for you, asking that you may be filled with the knowledge of his will in all spiritual wisdom and understanding, so as to walk in a manner worthy of the Lord, fully pleasing to him: bearing fruit in every good work and increasing in the knowledge of God; being strengthened with all power, according to his glorious might, for all endurance and patience with joy; giving thanks to the Father, who has qualified you to share in the inheritance of the saints in light. He has delivered us from the domain of darkness and transferred us to the kingdom of his beloved Son, in whom we have redemption, the forgiveness of sins.

Colossians 1:9-14

Praying For: __________

For this reason I bow my knees before the Father, from whom every family in heaven and on earth is named, that according to the riches of his glory he may grant you to be strengthened with power through his Spirit in your inner being, so that Christ may dwell in your hearts through faith—that you, being rooted and grounded in love, may have strength to comprehend with all the saints what is the breadth and length and height and depth, and to know the love of Christ that surpasses knowledge, that you may be filled with all the fullness of God.
Ephesians 3:14-19

Praying For: __________

Love is patient and kind; love does not envy or boast; it is not arrogant or rude. It does not insist on its own way; it is not irritable or resentful; it does not rejoice at wrongdoing, but rejoices with the truth. Love bears all things, believes all things, hopes all things, endures all things.
Love never ends. As for prophecies, they will pass away; as for tongues, they will cease; as for knowledge, it will pass away. For we know in part and we prophesy in part, but when the perfect comes, the partial will pass away.
When I was a child, I spoke like a child, I thought like a child, I reasoned like a child. When I became a man, I gave up childish ways. For now we see in a mirror dimly, but then face to face. Now I know in part; then I shall know fully, even as I have been fully known.
So now faith, hope, and love abide, these three; but the greatest of these is love.

1 Corinthians 13:4-13

Praying For: __________

SUCH IS THE CONFIDENCE THAT WE HAVE THROUGH CHRIST TOWARD GOD. NOT THAT WE ARE SUFFICIENT IN OURSELVES TO CLAIM ANYTHING AS COMING FROM US, BUT OUR SUFFICIENCY IS FROM GOD, WHO HAS MADE US SUFFICIENT TO BE MINISTERS OF A NEW COVENANT, NOT OF THE LETTER BUT OF THE SPIRIT. FOR THE LETTER KILLS, BUT THE SPIRIT GIVES LIFE.
2 CORINTHIANS 3:4-6

Praying For: __________

For if you forgive others their trespasses, your heavenly Father will also forgive you, but if you do not forgive others their trespasses, neither will your Father forgive your trespasses.

Matthew 6:14-15

Praying For: __________

For this reason, because I have heard of your faith in the Lord Jesus and your love toward all the saints, I do not cease to give thanks for you, remembering you in my prayers, that the God of our Lord Jesus Christ, the Father of glory, may give you the Spirit of wisdom and of revelation in the knowledge of him, having the eyes of your hearts enlightened, that you may know what is the hope to which he has called you, what are the riches of his glorious inheritance in the saints, and what is the immeasurable greatness of his power toward us who believe, according to the working of his great might that he worked in Christ when he raised him from the dead and seated him at his right hand in the heavenly places,

Ephesians 1:15-20

*Praying For:* __________

REJOICE IN THE LORD ALWAYS; AGAIN I WILL SAY, REJOICE. LET YOUR REASONA-BLENESS BE KNOWN TO EVERYONE. THE LORD IS AT HAND; DO NOT BE ANXIOUS ABOUT ANYTHING, BUT IN EVERYTHING BY PRAYER AND SUPPLICATION WITH THANKS-GIVING LET YOUR REQUESTS BE MADE KNOWN TO GOD. AND THE PEACE OF GOD, WHICH SURPASSES ALL UNDERSTAND-ING, WILL GUARD YOUR HEARTS AND YOUR MINDS IN CHRIST JESUS.

PHILIPPIANS 4:4-7

*Praying For:* __________

Put on then, as God's chosen ones, holy and beloved, compassionate hearts, kindness, humility, meekness, and patience, bearing with one another and, if one has a complaint against another, forgiving each other; as the Lord has forgiven you, so you also must forgive.

Colossians 3:12-13

*Praying For:* __________

Therefore, since we are surrounded by so great a cloud of witnesses, let us also lay aside every weight, and sin which clings so closely, and let us run with endurance the race that is set before us, looking to Jesus, the founder and perfecter of our faith, who for the joy that was set before him endured the cross, despis-ing the shame, and is seated at the right hand of the throne of God.

Hebrews 12:1-2

*Praying For:* __________

OH GIVE THANKS TO THE LORD, FOR HE IS GOOD; FOR HIS STEAD-FAST LOVE ENDURES FOREVER!

1 CHRONICLES 16:34

# CREATING A WAR ROOM

Do you have a special designated space in your home where you go to pray? If not, and you can, I encourage you to do so.

Establishing a specific space for prayer, sets this time with God apart and recognizes prayer as an important part of your life.

It doesn't require an extra room or any expense to set up your "War Room". Here are some tips to get started.

## 1 Designate a Space

Your War Room could be in a corner of your closet or in an extra closet. It could be an area in a guest bedroom, or even a chair in your living room. Maybe just a nightstand next to your bed. The size and location of the space is not what is important, but rather, the selecting of a specific spot to meet with God.

## 2 Repurpose your Space

You want to make your War Room space comfortable and inviting. Relocate items currently in your new prayer space, to another spot in your home. Gather all the items you might need during your prayer time like pens, pencils, note cards, etc. Have an area or wall which can be used to display scriptures, prayers and photos of friends and family members you want to pray over. Keep your Bible and a journal near so you can pray Scripture and take notes about your conversations with God.

## 3 Honor this Space

Commit to your new War Room as a space dedicated for one purpose—*prayer*. Limiting the use of this space for other activities will be a reminder to you and a witness to your family about the priority you place on spending time with God in prayer.

## 4 Prioritize time in your Prayer Space

Having a warm, inviting, inspiring space to talk to God is only helpful if you actual use it to meet with God. Schedule a specific time for prayer. Make a routine and establish the importance of this time alone with God. Be purposeful in designating a time which will allow you the maximum privacy, when you can shut out any distractions.

God longs to spend time with you soul friend, He is waiting for you to seek Him out.

DATE:

SCRIPTURE:

PRAISE:

FOR OTHERS:

## FOR ME:

## THANKSGIVING:

## GOD'S RESPONSE:

DATE:

SCRIPTURE:

PRAISE:

FOR OTHERS:

## FOR ME:

## THANKSGIVING:

## GOD'S RESPONSE:

DATE:

SCRIPTURE:

PRAISE:

FOR OTHERS:

## FOR ME:

## THANKSGIVING:

## GOD'S RESPONSE:

**DATE:**

**SCRIPTURE:**

**PRAISE:**

**FOR OTHERS:**

## FOR ME:

## THANKSGIVING:

## GOD'S RESPONSE:

DATE:

SCRIPTURE:

PRAISE:

FOR OTHERS:

## FOR ME:

## THANKSGIVING:

## GOD'S RESPONSE:

DATE:

SCRIPTURE:

PRAISE:

FOR OTHERS:

## FOR ME:

## THANKSGIVING:

## GOD'S RESPONSE:

DATE:

SCRIPTURE:

PRAISE:

FOR OTHERS:

## FOR ME:

## THANKSGIVING:

## GOD'S RESPONSE:

# PRAYER NEEDS

Name: ___

Need: ___

___

___

Name: ___

Need: ___

___

___

Name: ___

Need: ___

___

___

Name: ___

Need: ___

___

___

Name: ___

Need: ___

___

___

Name: ___

Need: ___

___

___

Name: ___

Need: ___

___

___

Name: ______________________________

Need: ______________________________

____________________________________

____________________________________

Name: ______________________________

Need: ______________________________

____________________________________

____________________________________

Name: ______________________________

Need: ______________________________

____________________________________

____________________________________

Name: ______________________________

Need: ______________________________

____________________________________

____________________________________

Name: ______________________________

Need: ______________________________

____________________________________

____________________________________

Name: ______________________________

Need: ______________________________

____________________________________

____________________________________

Name: ______________________________

Need: ______________________________

____________________________________

____________________________________

# PRAYER NEEDS

Name: ______________________________

Need: ______________________________

______________________________

______________________________

Name: ______________________________

Need: ______________________________

______________________________

______________________________

Name: ______________________________

Need: ______________________________

______________________________

______________________________

Name: ______________________________

Need: ______________________________

______________________________

______________________________

Name: ______________________________

Need: ______________________________

______________________________

______________________________

Name: ______________________________

Need: ______________________________

______________________________

______________________________

Name: ______________________________

Need: ______________________________

______________________________

______________________________

Name: ______________________________

Need: ______________________________

______________________________

______________________________

Name: ______________________________

Need: ______________________________

______________________________

______________________________

Name: ______________________________

Need: ______________________________

______________________________

______________________________

Name: ______________________________

Need: ______________________________

______________________________

______________________________

Name: ______________________________

Need: ______________________________

______________________________

______________________________

Name: ______________________________

Need: ______________________________

______________________________

______________________________

Name: ______________________________

Need: ______________________________

______________________________

______________________________

## *Jonah's Prayer*

Then Jonah prayed to the LORD his God
from the belly of the fish, saying,

**"I called out to the LORD, out of my distress,**
**and he answered me;**
**out of the belly of Sheol I cried,**
**and you heard my voice.**
**For you cast me into the deep,**
**into the heart of the seas,**
**and the flood surrounded me;**
**all your waves and your billows**
**passed over me.**
**Then I said, 'I am driven away**
**from your sight;**
**yet I shall again look**
**upon your holy temple.'**
**The waters closed in over me to take my life;**
**the deep surrounded me;**
**weeds were wrapped about my head**
**at the roots of the mountains.**
**I went down to the land**
**whose bars closed upon me forever;**
**yet you brought up my life from the pit,**
**O LORD my God.**
**When my life was fainting away,**
**I remembered the LORD,**
**and my prayer came to you,**
**into your holy temple.**
**Those who pay regard to vain idols**
**forsake their hope of steadfast love.**
**But I with the voice of thanksgiving**
**will sacrifice to you;**
**what I have vowed I will pay.**
**Salvation belongs to the LORD!"**

And the LORD spoke to the fish,
and it vomited Jonah out upon the dry land.

Jonah 2:1-10

# LORD, TEACH US TO PRAY

Can you imagine just for a moment being one of the twelve disciples. They gave up all they had to follow Jesus. With a single invitation, they stepped away from everything and everyone they knew to follow Jesus.

Can you imagine what they felt and thought as they witnessed first hand the miracles Jesus performed?

- Turning water to wine: John 2:1-11
- Healing the sick: Matthew 8:14-15
- Driving our evil spirits: Mark 1:21-27
- Raising the dead to life: Luke 7:11-17
- Calming stormy seas: Matthew 8:23-27
- Feeding the masses: John 6:1-15
- Walking on water: Mark 6:45-52

These are just a few of the 37 miracles of Jesus which are recorded in the New Testament.

I have read about these miracles, I have studied what the Bible has to say about them, but I have never witnessed Jesus standing in front of me literally making the wind and waves stop.

But His disciples did witness these things.

They also witnessed Jesus do something else. They watched Him go pray.

☐ Look up each of these Scriptures and notate what each reveals to us about Jesus' prayer habits.

☐ Mark 1:35

☐ Matthew 14:23

☐ Luke 6:12

☐ Luke 22:41

I am trying to imagine myself being there with Jesus and watching everything that He did. All those miracles out in the open, public for the crowds to see.

But this other thing He did—*prayer*– He left the disciples to pray on His own.

I think my curiosity would have gotten the best of me, I would want to know what Jesus was doing. I would also want to know how He prayed, how was it different from the prayers offered in the Temple by the High Priests?

So I actually do understand why, out of all the things the disciples witnessed Jesus do, the only thing they asked Him to teach them, was *how to pray.*

Jesus' response to his disciples inquiry was not intended to provide them with words to repeat each time they met with God in prayer, but rather He gave them principles to follow as they prayed.

*"Pray then like this:*
***Our Father in Heaven, hallowed be your name,***
***Your kingdom come, your will be done, on earth as it is in heaven.***
***Give us this day our daily bread, and forgive us our debts,***
***as we also have forgiven our debtors.***
***And lead us not into temptation, but deliver us from evil."***
Matthew 6:9-13

These principles of prayer are for us today also. Jesus, being our example in all things, is teaching us today just as he taught the twelve following him so closely during his earthly ministry.

Let's take a deeper look at the five principles of prayer Jesus has given to us.

## Offer Praise to God

*"Our Father in heaven, hallowed be your name."*

First and foremost, we pray to glorify God and recognize his sovereignty. Jesus tells his disciples to refer to God *His* Father, as God *their* father as well. Referring to God as our Father, conveys the authority, warmth and intimacy of a loving father. While "in heaven" reminds us of God's sovereign rule over all things. Jesus is inviting his disciples, and us, into the intimacy which Jesus shares with God the Father. However, we must always treat God with the highest of honor and recognize him as holy.

☐ How do each of the following scriptures support this? Write out each scripture then highlight, underline or circle the words which testify to God's holy nature.

1 Chronicles 16:25

Psalm 96:2

Isaiah 6:3

## 2 Guidance for God's Will

*"Your kingdom come, your will be done, on earth as it is in heaven"*

Christians are called to pray and work for the continual advancement of God's Kingdom on earth. This refers to Christ in the hearts of believers and in the body of the church. Praying for God's will instead of our own may be one of the most difficult prayers.

- [ ] Below is an excerpt of David's Psalm 25, "Teach Me Your Paths". Use the Verse Mapping study method, pg. 155, to extract the full meaning of each of these verses. Then notate your personal takeaway. The first verse has been completed as an example.

*Bountiful and gracious; God's divine character*

*A road, a course of life, mode of action*

8] Good and upright is the LORD;
therefore he instructs sinners in the way.

*To flow as water, to point out, to teach*

*A criminal, one accounted guilty — Me!!*

*Because God is good, He will always provide guidance and direction to even me.*

9] He leads the humble in what is right,
and teaches the humble his way.

10] All the paths of the LORD are steadfast love and faithfulness,
for those who keep his covenant and his testimonies.

## 3 NEEDS IN OUR LIFE

*"Give us this day our daily bread."*

God is our source to meet all of our physical needs and He is faithful to make this provision. Praying to Him for this provision, is an expression of our acknowledgment that we are completely dependent on Him to meet our physical needs as well as our spiritual needs. We can also intercede on other's behalf to petition God to meet their needs as well.

☐ Look up each of the following Scriptures, and notate how it speaks to you personally about God's provision in your own life.

2 Corinthians 9:10

Psalm 147:8

Matthew 6:26

Philippians 4:19

Psalm 72:12

Philippians 4:5-7

Proverbs 28:20

Proverbs 22:9

## Forgiveness

*"and forgive us our debts, as we also have forgiven our debtors."*

As believers, we are forgiven of our sin from the moment we receive God's saving grace, however because of our old nature, we continue to sin. The forgiveness Jesus is speaking of here is restorative. Sin separates. It causes a fracture in our relationship with God and it causes fractures in our relationships with each other. Once we understand what a great gift we have received from God through his forgiveness and restoration, we should be eager to forgive those in debt to us.

☐ Look up and read each Scripture in the list below. Then consider how you would answer each given question as it relates to that specific Scripture.

**1 John 1:9** > What does this Scripture reveal to you about God?

**Matthew 18:21-22** > How does this Scripture help you to see through God's eyes?

**Ephesians 4:31-33** > How can this Scripture help you grow Spiritually?

**Matthew 6:14-15** > How does this Scripture affect your relationship with God?

**Matthew 9:6** > What does this Scripture teach you about God's nature?

## 5 Deliverance from Sin

*"And lead us not into temptation, but deliver us from evil."*

We can be assured of this: trials and hardships will inevitably come to our lives. And while God never directly tempts us, He does sometimes lead us into situations to test us. In these times, we should pray to God for his deliverance. The best protection we have from sin and evil (temptation) is to turn to God and depend on his direction.

- ☐ How can the following Scriptures bring you hope in times of trials or temptation? Make a note how each could be applied to your personal prayer time.

**Psalm 41:4**

As for me, I said, "O LORD, be gracious to me; heal me, for I have sinned against you!"

---

**Psalm 103:2-4**

"Bless the LORD, O my soul, and forget not all his benefits, who forgives all your iniquity, who heals all your diseases, who redeems your life from the pit, who crowns you with steadfast love and mercy,"

---

**Psalm 6:2**

"Be gracious to me, O LORD, for I am languishing; heal me, O LORD, for my bones are troubled."

---

**Psalm 30:2**

"O LORD my God, I cried to you for help, and you have healed me."

---

**2 Kings 20:5**

"Turn back, and say to Hezekiah the leader of my people, Thus says the LORD, the God of David your father: I have heard your prayer; I have seen your tears. Behold, I will heal you. On the third day you shall go up to the house of the LORD, "

---

☐ Are you currently in the midst of a trial or battling temptation? Use the "Praying Scripture" method (pg. 69) and spend some time in prayer with God using one or several of the Scriptures on the previous page.

**DATE:**

**SCRIPTURE:**

**PRAISE:**

**FOR OTHERS:**

## FOR ME:

## THANKSGIVING:

## GOD'S RESPONSE:

DATE:

SCRIPTURE:

PRAISE:

FOR OTHERS:

## FOR ME:

## THANKSGIVING:

## GOD'S RESPONSE:

DATE:

SCRIPTURE:

PRAISE:

FOR OTHERS:

## FOR ME:

## THANKSGIVING:

## GOD'S RESPONSE:

DATE:

SCRIPTURE:

PRAISE:

FOR OTHERS:

## FOR ME:

## THANKSGIVING:

## GOD'S RESPONSE:

DATE:

SCRIPTURE:

PRAISE:

FOR OTHERS:

FOR ME:

THANKSGIVING:

GOD'S RESPONSE:

**DATE:**

**SCRIPTURE:**

**PRAISE:**

**FOR OTHERS:**

FOR ME:

THANKSGIVING:

GOD'S RESPONSE:

DATE:

SCRIPTURE:

PRAISE:

FOR OTHERS:

FOR ME:

THANKSGIVING:

GOD'S RESPONSE:

# PRAYER NEEDS

Name: ______________________________________________

Need: ______________________________________________

____________________________________________________

____________________________________________________

Name: ______________________________________________

Need: ______________________________________________

____________________________________________________

____________________________________________________

Name: ______________________________________________

Need: ______________________________________________

____________________________________________________

____________________________________________________

Name: ______________________________________________

Need: ______________________________________________

____________________________________________________

____________________________________________________

Name: ______________________________________________

Need: ______________________________________________

____________________________________________________

____________________________________________________

Name: ______________________________________________

Need: ______________________________________________

____________________________________________________

____________________________________________________

Name: ______________________________________________

Need: ______________________________________________

____________________________________________________

____________________________________________________

Name: ______________________________

Need: ______________________________

______________________________

______________________________

Name: ______________________________

Need: ______________________________

______________________________

______________________________

Name: ______________________________

Need: ______________________________

______________________________

______________________________

Name: ______________________________

Need: ______________________________

______________________________

______________________________

Name: ______________________________

Need: ______________________________

______________________________

______________________________

Name: ______________________________

Need: ______________________________

______________________________

______________________________

Name: ______________________________

Need: ______________________________

______________________________

______________________________

# PRAYER NEEDS

Name: ____________________

Need: ____________________

____________________

____________________

Name: ____________________

Need: ____________________

____________________

____________________

Name: ____________________

Need: ____________________

____________________

____________________

Name: ____________________

Need: ____________________

____________________

____________________

Name: ____________________

Need: ____________________

____________________

____________________

Name: ____________________

Need: ____________________

____________________

____________________

Name: ____________________

Need: ____________________

____________________

____________________

Name: ______________________________

Need: ______________________________

______________________________

______________________________

Name: ______________________________

Need: ______________________________

______________________________

______________________________

Name: ______________________________

Need: ______________________________

______________________________

______________________________

Name: ______________________________

Need: ______________________________

______________________________

______________________________

Name: ______________________________

Need: ______________________________

______________________________

______________________________

Name: ______________________________

Need: ______________________________

______________________________

______________________________

Name: ______________________________

Need: ______________________________

______________________________

______________________________

bless you

The Lord bless you
and keep you,

The Lord make his face
to shine upon you and
be gracious to you;

The Lord lift up his
countenance upon you
and give you peace.

Numbers 6:24-26

# PRAYING OVER YOUR HOME

## How would you define your home?

The dictionary app on my phone lists over two dozen definitions for the word "home".

I like this one *"the place in which one's domestic affections are centered."* Or how about, *"a principal base of operations or activities."* Although some days it does feel like *"one of three attack positions..".*

Whether it is large or small; owned, rented or borrowed; temporary or sort of permanent; new, old, or somewhere in-between; we all have some place we call home.

Home is our very personal private space. It's our family space. It's where real life happens with real life people feeling real feelings and fighting real battles.

If your home is like our home, we celebrate here, we play here, we cry here, we argue here, we contend here, we eat here, we entertain here, we learn here, we work here, we live life here everyday.

What place is more central to our lives than home?

So I want to invite you to do something you may have never done, or if you have, then I want to encourage you do it again - *pray over your home*.

There is really no specific way you have to do this, but I am going to share with you how I like to pray over my home.

## Let's take a prayer walk

A prayer walk is pretty simple, it is exactly what it says, *you pray as you walk*. I like to prayer walk around my neighborhood. It's a great stress reliever and helps me recenter.

But in this particular case, we are going to pray as we walk around our home.

"Our home" is where you live right now. It may be a 3 bdr, 3 bath in the burbs, it may be a one room apartment or space in the city. It may be a space on loan from a friend, or it may even be a place you don't really want to be. But we are going to walk all of these home places and spaces *together*.

We are each going to invite and welcome God into our homes. We are going to walk Him around our private spaces and talk to Him in those rooms.

To begin, we are going outside. Walk all the way around your house praying, not just for the physical structure but for all of your family and residents.

Then move inside, walking through each room praying for that room's purpose and family member. Pray for any specific needs of that person and your personal relationship with them, remembering to always include thanksgiving.

## 11 Scriptures to Pray Over Your Home

### WHOLE HOUSE

1. Dedicate your whole house and residents to God.

*"And if it is evil in your eyes to serve the LORD, choose this day whom you will serve, whether the gods your fathers served in the region beyond the River, or the gods of the Amorites in whose land you dwell.* ***But as for me and my house, we will serve the LORD****."* Joshua 24:15

### FOUNDATION

2. Build your family's spiritual foundation on God.

*"He is like a man building a house, who dug deep and laid the foundation on the rock. And when a flood arose, the stream broke against that house and could not shake it, because it had been well built."* Luke 6:48

### FRONT DOOR / ENTRY

3. Protection from the outside world.

*"He has made strong the iron bands of your doors; he has sent blessings on your children inside your walls."* Psalm 147:13 (BBE)

### FAMILY ROOM

4. The building of unity and healthy relationships.

*"Put on then, as God's chosen ones, holy and beloved, compassionate hearts, kindness, humility, meekness, and patience, bearing with one another and, if one has a complaint against another, forgiving each other; as the Lord has forgiven you, so you also must forgive. And above all these put on love, which binds everything together in perfect harmony. And let the peace of Christ rule in your hearts, to which indeed you were called in one body. And be thankful. Let the word of Christ dwell in you richly, teaching and admonishing one another in all wisdom, singing psalms and hymns and spiritual songs, with thankfulness in your hearts to God. And whatever you do, in word or deed, do everything in the name of the Lord Jesus, giving thanks to God the Father through him."* Colossians 3:12-17

### KITCHEN

5. Create a welcoming environment for others.

*"Contribute to the needs of the saints and seek to show hospitality."* Romans 12:13

### Dining Area

6. Bless the food and share with others.

*"He took the seven loaves and the fish, and having given thanks he broke them and gave them to the disciples, and the disciples gave them to the crowds."* Matthew 15:36

### Bathrooms

7. Pray for good health and well being.

*"Beloved, I pray that all may go well with you and that you may be in good health, as it goes well with your soul."* 3 John 1:2

### Master Bedroom

8. Develop a harmonious marital relationship.

*"With all humility and gentleness, with patience, bearing with one another in love, eager to maintain the unity of the Spirit in the bond of peace."* Ephesians 4:2-3

### Children's Bedroom

9. Teach your children to follow God.

*"Teach me your way, O LORD, that I may walk in your truth; unite my heart to fear your name."* Psalm 86:11

### Guest Bedroom

10. A blessing for peace.

*"The LORD bless you and keep you; the LORD make his face to shine upon you and be gracious to you; the LORD lift up his countenance upon you and give you peace."* Numbers 6:24-26

### Office or Work Space

11. Dedicate your work to God.

*"Whatever you do, work heartily, as for the Lord and not for men, knowing that from the Lord you will receive the inheritance as your reward. You are serving the Lord Christ."* Colossians 3:23-24

DATE:

SCRIPTURE:

PRAISE:

FOR OTHERS:

## FOR ME:

## THANKSGIVING:

## GOD'S RESPONSE:

DATE:

SCRIPTURE:

PRAISE:

FOR OTHERS:

FOR ME:

THANKSGIVING:

GOD'S RESPONSE:

DATE:

SCRIPTURE:

PRAISE:

FOR OTHERS:

FOR ME:

THANKSGIVING:

GOD'S RESPONSE:

DATE:

SCRIPTURE:

PRAISE:

FOR OTHERS:

## FOR ME:

## THANKSGIVING:

## GOD'S RESPONSE:

DATE:

SCRIPTURE:

PRAISE:

FOR OTHERS:

FOR ME:

THANKSGIVING:

GOD'S RESPONSE:

DATE:

SCRIPTURE:

PRAISE:

FOR OTHERS:

FOR ME:

THANKSGIVING:

GOD'S RESPONSE:

DATE:

SCRIPTURE:

PRAISE:

FOR OTHERS:

## FOR ME:

## THANKSGIVING:

## GOD'S RESPONSE:

# PRAYER NEEDS

Name: ______________________________________________

Need: ______________________________________________

____________________________________________________

____________________________________________________

Name: ______________________________________________

Need: ______________________________________________

____________________________________________________

____________________________________________________

Name: ______________________________________________

Need: ______________________________________________

____________________________________________________

____________________________________________________

Name: ______________________________________________

Need: ______________________________________________

____________________________________________________

____________________________________________________

Name: ______________________________________________

Need: ______________________________________________

____________________________________________________

____________________________________________________

Name: ______________________________________________

Need: ______________________________________________

____________________________________________________

____________________________________________________

Name: ______________________________________________

Need: ______________________________________________

____________________________________________________

____________________________________________________

Name: ______________________________

Need: ______________________________

______________________________

______________________________

Name: ______________________________

Need: ______________________________

______________________________

______________________________

Name: ______________________________

Need: ______________________________

______________________________

______________________________

Name: ______________________________

Need: ______________________________

______________________________

______________________________

Name: ______________________________

Need: ______________________________

______________________________

______________________________

Name: ______________________________

Need: ______________________________

______________________________

______________________________

Name: ______________________________

Need: ______________________________

______________________________

______________________________

# PRAYER NEEDS

Name: ____________________

Need: ____________________

____________________

____________________

Name: ____________________

Need: ____________________

____________________

____________________

Name: ____________________

Need: ____________________

____________________

____________________

Name: ____________________

Need: ____________________

____________________

____________________

Name: ____________________

Need: ____________________

____________________

____________________

Name: ____________________

Need: ____________________

____________________

____________________

Name: ____________________

Need: ____________________

____________________

____________________

Name: ______________________________

Need: ______________________________

______________________________

______________________________

Name: ______________________________

Need: ______________________________

______________________________

______________________________

Name: ______________________________

Need: ______________________________

______________________________

______________________________

Name: ______________________________

Need: ______________________________

______________________________

______________________________

Name: ______________________________

Need: ______________________________

______________________________

______________________________

Name: ______________________________

Need: ______________________________

______________________________

______________________________

Name: ______________________________

Need: ______________________________

______________________________

______________________________

*Verse Mapping Example: Psalm 25:8*

Bountiful and gracious; God's divine character

A road, a course of life, mode of action

8] Good and upright is the LORD;

therefore he instructs sinners in the way.

To flow as water, to point out, to teach

A criminal, one accounted guilty -- Me!!

Because God is good, He will always provide guidance and direction to even me.

# VERSE MAPPING

If you are not already familiar with the Bible Study method of Verse Mapping, let me introduce you to one of my favorite study methods.

**VERSE MAPPING DRAWS US DEEPER INTO THE WORD OF GOD AS WE PAUSE OUR READING AND LOOK AT EACH WORD AND PHRASE OF A SCRIPTURE TO EXTRACT A BETTER UNDERSTANDING OF THESE HOLY TEXTS.**

First, know that there is NOT a wrong way to do this. The purpose of the exercise is to wring every little bit of meaning an application our of a Scripture. Picture, if you will, a wet towel being folded over and twisted tight to release all of the water being held. Twisted and wrung until the very last drop has been extracted. This is how we want to extract from Scripture, what God has to teach us.

Second, while the writing portion of verse mapping is focused on a single, or small selection of Scripture, know that the study process goes well beyond a single Scripture reference.

## LET'S GET STARTED

Referencing the example provided, use the blank space to the left for your own workspace.

1. **Select the Scripture** to map.
2. **Read the verse**, praying to God for Him to give you understanding.
3. **Write out the verse.** Leave plenty of space around it, between the lines and between the words.
4. **Personalize it.** If applicable, replace words like you, we, us, them with your own name.
5. **Mark, circle, underline, highlight words and phrases** that stand out to you.
    - Any words make you want to dig deeper? Look up and define any words which need clarification.
    - Any promises from or actions of God?
    - Any action encouraged or required on your part?
6. **Read the verse in context.** Read the preceding and following verses or whole chapter. See how it ties in to the verses before and after it.
7. **Read the verse in other translations.** Note which words or phrases help you understand or apply the verse.
8. **Cross-reference the verse.** Find, list and read other verses which speak about the same topic.
9. **Notate your take-a-way.** What is God teaching you through this Bible verse?

Finally, don't be afraid to ask yourself, "what does this mean?" then go researching. Use Bible study tools and resources to help you dig deeper. (Try BibleHub.com or BibleStudyTools.com) Set aside anything you already know about the verse, look for information and explanations which you did not know. But mostly, be open and listen to what God wants to teach you.

# DO YOU KNOW JESUS?

God loves us so much that He sent His Son, Jesus, to die on the cross to pay the price for our sins and bring us into a relationship with Him. (John 3:16) Through Christ, we can know the promise of eternal life and experience the joy of knowing God here on earth!

If you would like to have a relationship with God, the Bible tells us that the first step is acknowledging that we have sinned and that there is nothing we can do to earn God's love (Romans 3:23-26). Next, we believe and confess that Jesus is Lord (Romans 10:9) and allow Him to guide our lives.

Where we once wanted to control our own future, we now invite Jesus into our hearts to be Lord over our lives.

Knowing God's peace, perspective and purpose for your life begins with a personal relationship with Jesus.

Would you like to accept Jesus as Lord of your life? You can pray the following prayer:

*Lord, I confess that I have sinned against You and ask You to forgive me. I'm sorry that my sin has hurt You and other people in my life. I acknowledge that I could never earn salvation by my good works, but I come to You and trust in what Jesus did for me on the cross.*

*I believe that You love me and that Jesus died and rose again so that I can be forgiven and come to know You. I ask You to come into my heart and be Lord of my life. I trust You with everything, and I thank You for loving me so much that I can know You here on earth and spend the rest of eternity with You in heaven.*

*In Jesus name, Amen*

# OTHER GREAT RESOURCES

From Sweet To The Soul Ministries

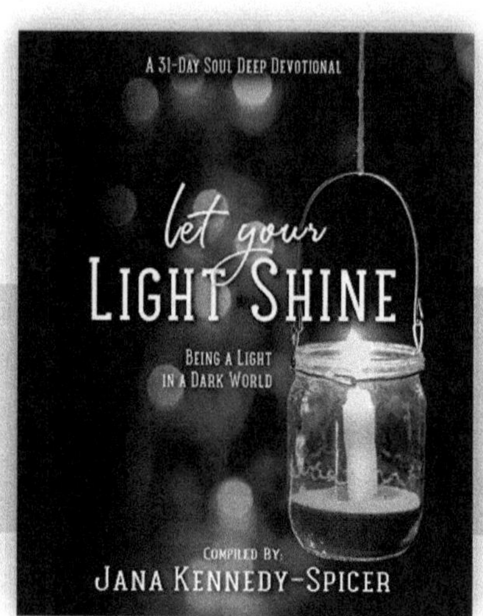


**LET YOUR LIGHT SHINE**

We live in a dark world, and it seems to be getting darker day by day. Fear, depression, grief, abuse, illness can seem overwhelming. But there is hope. There is a light. *Let Your Light Shine* is a 31-day journey through God's Word to learn about the hope we have in Christ Jesus.

**GRACIOUS WORDS**

James warns us that the tongue is small but mighty. The ability to control our tongues and our words comes only through surrendering them to God and allowing the Holy Spirit to intercede. It takes great obedience on our part to keep our words gracious.

**REVIVE US AGAIN**

We live in a broken and fallen world, but recent events have left many of us feeling despair and seeking God for revival, like never before. *Revive Us Again* is 31 day Scripture Study Journal which includes journaling / study scripture prompts to help us learn more about the revival we seek.

**PRAYING FOR REVIVAL**

At times we can feel beaten and broken by life. But we have a God who loves us and longs to bring restoration and revival. *Praying for Revival,* is a 40 day Prayer Journal which includes scripture based prayer prompts to guide us as we pray for the revival we seek.

# INSPIRING WOMEN
## WHO THEY ARE & HOW TO BE ONE

Learn about Biblical examples of inspiring women

Hear personal testimony from friends about the inspiring women in their lives

Study 31 Biblical Characteristics of an Inspiring Woman

**There's not an age requirement to being an Inspiring Woman,
but yet I feel now some ownership of this responsibility.
Had it not been for the Inspiring Women in my life,
where would I be today?**

**~ Jana Kennedy-Spicer**

VISIT SWEETTOTHESOUL.COM/INSPIRING-WOMEN FOR INFORMATION

# VISIT US ON-LINE

SweetToTheSoul.com

SweetToTheSoulShoppe.com

**SOUL INSPIRED SCRIPTURE READING PLANS:** Each month consists of a topic-driven reading plan, complete with 31 Scriptures to use in your Bible study and quiet time. The verses serve as a guide to dive deep into God's Word as you focus on small portions. Blank Scripture Journal pages are also available for download.

**SOUL INSPIRED BIBLE STUDY RESOURCES:** Soul Inspired Bible Study is about spending time in the scripture with God and allowing the Holy Spirit to give us understanding. These Bible Studies cover a variety of topics and offer resources in multiple formats including journals, devotionals and more.

**INSPIRED INBOX:** These free Soul Inspired Bible Studies are delivered directly to your inbox. Choose from several topics. Just sign up, check your email box, then download and print all your study materials. Study alone at your own pace or invite friends to join you and study the Bible together.

**SOUL INSPIRED BIBLE JOURNALING RESOURCES:** are designed to inspire your soul and encourage you to use your creativity during your Bible Study time. Our journaling resources include Bible Journaling Kits, printable templates / colorable bookmarks, coloring pages, scripture cards and more!

**SOUL INSPIRED COLORING BOOKS:** Coloring is a wonderful way to relax and destress. Our coloring books include inspirational Scripture and encouraging quotes through beautifully hand-drawn artwork. Be inspired as you spend time reflecting on scripture as well as enjoying the calming and refreshing benefits of coloring.

**SWEET TO THE SOUL SHOPPE:** Our on-line shoppe is where you will find all of our Bible Journaling and creative resources. Many resources are printable instant digital downloads.
We also have several sets of scripture cards and blank encouragement cards.
Visit sweettothesoulshoppe.com to see our full line of products.

Our Bible Studies and Journals are available for purchase via Amazon.
Visit sweettothesoul.com for direct links to each of our books or journals.

# MEET OUR AUTHORS

## Jana Kennedy Spicer

**JANA KENNEDY SPICER**, Founder of *Sweet To The Soul Ministries*, is a wife, mom and Nana. She is a born and raised Texas girl who loves boots, sunflowers and sweet tea. She has a heart for studying God's Word and is passionate about encouraging women to do the same.

After a 30 year corporate career, God called her to share her art and love of Bible Study with others. Her favorite part of ministry is where her faith and art collide! This is the sweet spot where souls become inspired.

She is the author of *Let Your Light Shine: Being a Light in a Dark World* and *Gracious Words: Speaking with Kindness and Mercy*; and the illustrator of the scripture based *Garden of Life Coloring Book* and *Coloring the Scriptures.*

You can follow Jana on Instagram @ jana_sweettothesoul and Facebook @Sweet.To.The.Soul.Ministries

Follow her Bible Journaling and creative arts on Facebook and Instagram @SweetToTheSoulShoppe

## Betsy de Cruz

**BETSY DE CRUZ** helps overwhelmed women take small steps to invite more of God's presence and power into their lives. Connect with Betsy to get your free Quiet Time Renewal Guide and other resources at FaithSpillingOver.com. Her book *More of God* is a distracted woman's guide to more meaningful quiet times. After living in the Middle East for 16 years with her husband and two children, Betsy landed in Texas, where she still enjoys drinking chai with friends.

# END NOTES

**Introduction**

Before Amen, by Max Lucado
Published by Thomas Nelson, Nashville, Tennessee, 2014

When You Pray Big Things Happen, by Karmen Smith
Published independently, BlessingsBeyondTheBarnyard.com

**Propelled to Pray**

ESV (English Standard Version) Study Bible
Published by Crossway Bibles, Wheaton, Illnoic, 2008

SWEETTOTHESOUL.com

www.ingramcontent.com/pod-product-compliance
Lightning Source LLC
LaVergne TN
LVHW080331110826
845155LV00024B/145

* 9 7 8 1 9 5 3 7 1 8 0 4 4 *